Nothing is Real

Nothing is Real

Fact and Photography

Bart van Leeuwen

© 2015 Bart van Leeuwen
Translation: Django van Leeuwen and Molly Holmes

Cover, Photography and Design: Bart van Leeuwen
Elegance Magazine, Trentino Italy 1993
Models: Jaime and Joanna
Styling and Production: Maarten Spruyt
Hair and Make-up: Clark Accord

CreateSpace
ISBN-13: 978-1532869839
ISBN-10: 1532869835

Content

1. Fact and Photography

Not long after I had seen the photographs in *The Family of Man,* the book about the exhibition in the MoMA, curated by Edward Steichen, my mother bought me my first camera.
A little box with a lens. "To keep me off the streets".
I must have been twelve or thirteen years old.
She probably noticed how the book with 'the man with the flute' on the cover fascinated me, probably in the same way it had fascinated the nine million people who would eventually visit the exhibition it belonged to.
I went through it over and over again.
What I liked so much about it was that the expression of emotions of the people in the pictures, despite their diversity in looks, culture and habitat, was apparently the same, all over the world, universal. Sadness was sadness, happiness happiness, compassion compassion. It was clear there were more similarities than differences between all those people

and nations, regardless of where and how they lived and what they looked like.

It made me enthusiastic about life and the world we were living in and I became aware of something which was hard for me as a child to describe, but connected us all; humanity.

I started to look at things differently and was able to understand people better.

The Family of Man has probably been the inspiration for all of my later work in which, conscious or not, I was always looking for a timeless, universal human story, be it fashion, portrait, advertising or documentary photography.

The first pictures I made with my little camera – a fruit bowl with some apples and pears, my little sister on the bridge in front of our house and some homeless people on a park bench – I developed with the help of Sjoerd Holsbergen, a family friend. He was a couple of years older than I was, interested in becoming a photographer himself, and acquainted with some of the hip Dutch photographers of those days. But most of all the proud owner of a real darkroom. Sjoerd's younger sister, Sybilla, had covered the walls of her room from floor to ceiling with pictures of William Klein, Irving Penn and Richard Avedon. Pictures from *Vogue* that were reflecting the times we were living in, in a way I had not seen before, the way I felt it.

While my first rolls of film were in the fixing bath in the well equipped darkroom of my photographer friend, Bob Dylan's *Subterranean Homesick Blues* sounded from the speakers. All I could see was the little green light of an amplifier.

I thought it was fascinating: first of all photography itself - making images of things that interested me from angles and in a light chosen by me – and now this whole process of developing and fixing the negatives, with unknown chemicals, all of it taking place in the dark, and then, the music. Altogether it was *magical*.

A couple of days later, after the films had dried, we made some proofs and right from the beginning I noticed that the framed reality on the contact sheets had more content, importance and maybe even more poetry, than the original *actual* reality.

The fruit in the bowl looked more fruity, more desirable, my sister looked more insecure than she liked to see herself, and the shopping bag people more sad than you would expect from a distance.

I realized that there can be much importance and beauty in ostensibly small, unnoticeable things, which, when captured in the right light, at the right moment and within the right frame, suddenly becomes visible and gives content and meaning to a subject. The motion of a hand, a frown, a sultry look, a child dancing with its own shadow, fallen leaves blown by the wind.

Later when I read *The Devil's Drool* by the Argentinean author Julio Cortazar, I recognized this. In this short story Cortazar gives the best possible definition of photography that I've heard to this day: "One of the best ways of combating oblivion and nothingness, is taking photographs..." "Nothingness" as Cortazar worded it: "That rough and delicious career of sunlight on an old stone, or the dancing braids of a girl returning with a loaf or a bottle of milk..." When you look at things, or better *see* things, this way and have an eye for casual, seemingly insignificant, ephemeral things, existence itself seems to have more content, more beauty and meaning, causing you to be grabbed and shaken by the simple and the mundane.

This way I found out that photography was not only a means to register reality but, first of all, a tool to show others what *I* saw. How *I* experienced things. A way to express or accentuate all kind of ideas and emotions, put things in a certain light. Little things, sometimes, that you're not always aware of, but which are essential for a fully conscious existence. That it was possible, like in poetry, to transmit feelings that are hard to describe, but give a deeper meaning which can be understood by others and I understood that photographers can do with images what writers can do with words.

To be a photographer seemed like a great profession.

Once I had discovered these means of expression - the fact that nothing was *as subjective as an objective* - and it had become clear to me that photography was the preferred medium to give importance to seemingly unnoticeable things, I understood that the opposite had to be true as well. That no other medium would be able to give such a distorted, exaggerated or even completely false impression of a situation, create feigned sentiments in such a flawless way or show people and circumstances totally differently from the way they are.

Appearances are deceptive, nothing is what it seems, *that* I already knew, but that it was expressed so clearly through photography was something new to me.

Because of this subjectivity, photography appears to have little to do with reality. Photography, however, is able to produce an image which *resembles* reality; something which professionals in particular make use of. This is in direct contrast to common perceptions, i.e. that photography actually *portrays* reality.

"Photographs don't lie," Lewis Hine said at the beginning of the twentieth century, "but liars may photograph!"

Hine made an effort to improve the social position of the lower classes. When he photographed a New York slum, some hundred years ago, you could be sure the whole neighborhood would be torn down within no time, because he was perfectly able to depict the essence of what he wanted to show by focusing on the poverty of the people and the lack of maintenance of the buildings they were living in.

Photography is concerned with more than capturing reality at a certain point in time. The act of framing a small section of the real world seems to add an importance over and above the original piece of reality, lifting it out of the ordinary, like adding an extra dimension.

That extra dimension, that deeper meaning can be present in the subject of the image itself, but it is also possible to experience something which is not visible within the frame, when the story that is told extends beyond the borders of the photograph; through association, symbolism or atmosphere, which makes a picture more interesting.

Photographers use lighting, framing, focus, direction and choice of moment in their efforts to create that extra dimension. In that manner they 'construct' images, give shape to their vision; be that universal ideas, your own fantasy or the product of somebody else's imagination, rational or intuitional does not matter. Some do it after long nights of brainstorming, others on the fly, in a split second.

Not long after I had developed my first films in my friend's darkroom, I saw Antonioni's film *BlowUp* - based on Cortázar's story - in which the protagonist struggles with the uncertainty about to which degree the images he creates are objective and represent reality - something that fitted perfectly with my 'discovery' - something became clear to me. After Steichen and *the Family of Men* and the intriguing black and white pictures of Avedon, Klein and Penn – who represented our present days and were timeless and universal at the same time – *BlowUp* took my last feelings of doubt away.

I enjoyed painting and writing short stories for the school magazine, but to be able to interpret reality, to make things look real and show them to others, *as I saw them,* seemed like an even more beautiful profession to me than being a painter or a writer.

I wanted to become a photographer.

2. Form and Content

So photography turned out to be a subjective interpretation of the world around us, the reflection of a personal reality. A tool you can use to show others what *you* are seeing, what *you* think of the subject photographed, a tool you can use to show *a personal* vision; one of the fundamental elements of good photography. In the first place it is *vision* that makes it possible for photographers to distinguish themselves from others. A particular talent for that will certainly help.

To create images without vision, merely well exposed and in focus – such as a picture of a chocolate bar in an ad - is easy to learn for most of us, either in amateur classes or schools for professional photography. In that case we are talking about pictures *of* its subject instead of pictures *about* its subject. Maybe beautiful and well *designed*, but neutral registrations that immediately show the spectators what they're dealing with. Functional but uninteresting. They only show what the subject looks like, not what it represents. They might trigger your imagination and maybe stir something within you or make you *think*, but that's due to your own imagination, and not to the vision of the photographer.

The criterion for whether such a pure registering picture - meant for stocktaking, identification, or as a memory aid, intended to be used in a passport, catalogue or personnel administration – is valid or not is if you are be able to recognize the depicted item the moment you see it.

If you think: "Ah, a bar of chocolate." Then the picture is ok. In this case a personal signature is unimportant, undesirable even.

But when the chocolate is photographed with a certain vision, in a way, for instance, that makes you want 'to crawl into the chocolate', or pieces of chocolate are positioned in a pattern which is attractive to the eye, it is possible that someone who doesn't even like chocolate might succumb to it after all.

To create neutral photographic registrations without commitment or vision is a profession in itself. Perhaps a passport photo machine or surveillance camera will be capable of doing so. Personally I think it's impossible.

Extremely boring anyway; even the pictures of industrial sites and mining installations, like gas tanks and winding towers by German photographers Bernd en Hilla Becher - pictures that lack every kind of emotion and are as attractive to me as a catalogue for vacuum cleaners or plumber tools, but are held in high esteem in the world of arts – are not pure objective registrations. The photographers have systematically put their subjects in the same kind of light and chosen a similar point of view. Consistently trying to avoid coincidence and subjectivity in turn creates subjectivity.

It never impressed me very much but I know a lot of people love it.

To make pictures that arouse the interest of the spectator when used as a means of communication, you should in the first place be concerned with making sure that the photograph shows something that has a certain meaning or importance in the eyes of the spectator, something that fires the imagination. In other words: a picture needs a context which can be clearly felt or understood.

The more this context coincides with universal, human feelings – humanity – the more one will sense or understand what the picture is about without any further explanation. This interpretation is not always unambiguous, however, and may differ from person to person. Especially because, as we've seen before, it's possible that emotions arise from things that are not visible within the frame but the result of suggestion or association. The deeper layer.

To reach a large audience the subject of a picture, the content, the story that is told, has to be credible. As uncontrived, unaffected, unstudied and un-posed possible. Not *visibly* fictitious, made-up with the idea of creating an outstanding image. This has an unnatural effect that will only be understood and appreciated by a limited, already niche audience. It is feasible, of course, to fabricate something in order to create a more interesting image concerning form or content; for many of us the reason for taking up photography. However, similarly to film, you shouldn't *be aware* of it. As soon as you can *see* that a picture is contrived, it alienates itself from the viewer, loses its credibility, and demands to be seen as 'art'.

When it is clear that a picture is made with the idea to impress, by, for instance, emotion and when this emotion is *visibly* artificially raised by mise-en scène or posing, which makes you conscious of the fact you're looking at something that pretends to be something that it is *not* - a picture made to show emotion instead of an emotional picture - the feeling disappears. The photograph will look fake, cheesy and we are dealing with kitsch. Just like the tricks of a magician. They need to be incomprehensible to be taken seriously.

When we're dealing with an outstanding subject and the context can only be understood by spectators who are familiar with the subject or when one has to read what the picture is about in a separate booklet, it cannot be seen as a universal means of communication. This makes it very ineffective, in spite of its possible illustrative powers. Unless the description is short and powerful it indicates that the photographs are meant for small, selected audiences only.

If a writer already has to adhere to: "Show, don't tell", what kind of photographer are you – creator of images - if you have to explain your pictures? The fact that a picture itself shows what it is about is the essence of good photography and a photographer's craftsmanship.

Apart from being meaningful in content, pictures must be strong in form. Form generates attention for content. Both elements are necessary for a good picture. No form without content, no content without form.

In the first place pictures have to be aesthetically pleasing. "They have to be pleasing to the eye." is what Kathy Ryan, director of photography of *The New York Times*, said, recently. I agree.

Of course *beauty* is a subjective concept depending on fashion; "in the eye of the beholder" as Plato said; and in spite of an ever changing beauty ideal, I think in the first place of beauty as we recognize it from the history of art and music, or of what John Keats was referring to in his *Endymion*:

A thing of beauty is a joy forever
Its loveliness will never
Pass into nothingness: but still will keep
A bower quiet for us, and a sleep
Full of sweet dreams...

With regard to photography, the description of 'beautiful' as found in most dictionaries, is sufficient as well: "nice, pretty, handsome, lovely, charming, good-looking, attractive, enchanting, entrancing, fair, kind, fine". Harmonious could be added, but since we are talking about photography, my first choice would be *good to look at.* Who wants to look at ugliness, or listen to a terrible noise?

One way or the other, photographs have to be aesthetic.

Apart from exciting, they must be at least harmonious, regarding composition, clair obscure, and colour.

This is something many photographers feel intuitively but it's also something many books have been written about, usually referring to - in this case very comparably - drawing or painting.

Flat pictures, pictures without any composition, or composed as a *currant bun* are dull, don't attract the eye. That's why – unless you prefer flat and dull – you should look for lines and shapes, negative space and simplification to create depth and tension.

Many different *screaming* colours express something restless, jittery, add an unbalanced feel to a picture. Try to avoid them by framing or isolation. If that doesn't work then use it, by exaggerating the effect; or use black and white.

In the case of news gathering it can be necessary to photograph ugly or shocking, disturbing things. In this instance it would be in bad taste to depict this horror with a sense of *beauty*, which would also detract from the credibility of the photographs and the situations shown on them.

A low-key approach is what I suggest, as objective and realistic possible. Low points of view, dramatic foregrounds – think of burning tires, lost toys or a single shoe – are often used in war pictures to give this kind of photography extra impact. Smoke and bad weather conditions also strongly influence the dramatic effect of a picture.

Newspapers, TV, and internet confront us on a daily basis with all kinds of hardship and cruelty that exists all around us. Hatred, fear, envy, hunger, greed, aggression, adversity, incomprehension, it's everywhere.

Apart from the fact that I'm sure I'm unable emotionally to work in that field, it suits my character better to try to discover beauty in the chaos that surrounds us, than to regularly show by means of pictures – how important that might be – how much sorrow exists.

I always preferred to photograph and show harmonious things that inspire positive thoughts, instead of showing the dark side over and over again.

Beauty, to me, is a necessity, closely related to consolation.

During the 20s and 30s of the last century, an exploration of the expressive possibilities of the then relatively new medium of photography related to the art of painting originated.

This often resulted in a form of photography which was characterized by solarisation, double images, shadows and negative space, pictures that were basically abstractions of reality. Form was the fundament, content came second. Photographers from that period like André Kertész, László Moholy-Nagy, Alexander Rodchenko and Man Ray are still famous for their *new* ways of seeing.

This type of work was the trend in *art photography* during the 40s and 50s but, became *old-fashioned* when John Szarkowski, Director of Photography at the MoMA in New York, developed his *Mirrors and Windows* theory in the late 70s. By *Mirrors* he meant the expression of pure personal ideas and emotions, by *Windows* the subjective depicting of the visible reality. "It isn't what a picture is of, it's what a picture is about", is how Szarkowski defined the essence of modern photography.

This meant the end of the traditional nineteenth century point of view that what you see in a picture is *real*, that it is showing the truth or reality, which started the era of 'snapshot aesthetics' with committed photographers like Diane Arbus, Robert Frank, Jaques Henri Lartique, William Klein and Gary Winogrand. Ed van der Elsken, Johan van der Keuken, Martin Parr and the recently *discovered* Vivian Maier would have fit perfectly into this list.

This new insight - which meant that a photographer could distinguish himself from others, not only by form but also by content and vision, or as Szarkowski stated it: 'To quote out of context is the essence of the photographer's craft." - caused a change in appreciation of photography from *Mirrors* (Ray, Kertész) to *Windows* (Arbus, Frank, Winogrand), while today, fifty years later, it looks like if we are seeing a slow change in the direction of *Mirrors* again (Van Lamsweerde – Matadin, Tim Walker), which quite ironically, probably has to do with the fact that one has become used to digital techniques and the newly evolved knowledge that what you see in a picture is not *the* truth but just a subjective representation of reality. Something which, of course, has been like that since the very beginning.

Photographic techniques employed can be determining factors, for form as well as for content.

One of the specific characteristics of modern photography is the possibility to depict a unique, once-only moment, razor-sharp, a facility that, for technical reasons, didn't exist in the early days of the medium. Besides the sensitivity of the early photographic materials, which is incomparable to the today's equipment, lenses were not as fast as they are now. Blurred pictures, due to long exposure times and moving subjects, were common things and could only be avoided by means of not moving at all for several seconds in order to avoid being depicted as a foggy shade.

As a result of that we are all familiar with the static, posed, pictures which, in combination with their typical sepia tone, were characteristic of the photographs in those days.

When the negative materials became more sensitive and the lenses faster - which resulted in the possibility to photograph moving subjects as *frozen* - we were able to depict a very different image of reality than hundred years ago.

Nowadays there is an virtually infinite choice of available technical possibilities, but it will always remain a tool for realizing what photography is actually about: vision and, finally, communication.

Besides today's plethora of digital cameras - which replaced many of the analogue ones, but are very comparable considering it being a tool to capture a vision – you now find lenses and technical possibilities which draw a sharper picture than the human eye, which causes a kind of hyperrealism that shows us an image which is *more realistic than reality.*

Some people love this while others are reintroducing the hundred and fifty years old *Wet Plate Collodion Process* with a completely different effect.

A couple of years ago the *Red*, a new kind of camera was introduced – a digital camera which makes it possible to shoot photographs like 35 mm film: up to 60 frames a second at high shutter-speeds and with a high resolution.

Afterwards, just like an art director, you can chose the right moment, by which in fact the *decisive* moment is postponed.

Through modern, advanced computer techniques it is currently possible to create photomontages which one could only dream of in earlier days. Halfway through the nineteenth century the head of president Abraham Lincoln was simply cut out and glued to the body of former vice-president John Calhoun; now we see models climb buildings like insects, pop stars with three heads that look at each other, and waggish babies with moustaches knocking about.

Like anything else, also photography is subject to fashion. I'm very curious as to what's next.

In the meantime the essence doesn't change.

When I see a picture that tells it's story well, pleases the eye and gives the impression that what I see really happened and is not *constructed* for the sake of the photograph itself, I think we're moving towards what I consider to be *a good shot*. This happens particularly when the image expresses a unique moment as well as when what is happening in the shot touches you emotionally or rationally, triggers your fantasy or raises a question that'll make you think.

By additionally capturing a universal view of mankind, in which emotions have throughout history always stayed the same play a part, an everlasting timeless feel arises, an image that will hardly be influenced by clothing or décor.

In pictures like that it will be *forever now*.

For free work as well for assignments, this is the kind of style I always tried to hold on to and which pleases me the most; to create as well as to look at.

3. People and Their Surroundings

Apart from the subjectivity aroused by a photographer's vision, I sometimes ask myself to what extend we can talk about a representation of *reality* when photographing people.

Most people change their behaviour when they become aware of the presence of a camera or see a *Smartphone* pointed at them and find it difficult to continue with what they were doing as soon as they realize they will be frozen in time, for the world to see.

Some make exaggerated gestures indicating they don't want to be photographed and turn their head away, but it strikes me every time again, how many people start to pose, put on airs and act differently from the way they are.

They start to make funny faces or look seriously or gracefully into the camera. Some put on sunglasses or a weird little hat, others hold up an object.

Normally nice people suddenly start clowning around, acting like fools. They try to look sexier, tougher, funnier, better, whatever, in order to give an impression of themselves different from what they think they look like.

Nothing new in itself. Behaviour like that already existed long before the digital age in which we always have a camera at hand, and many claim their 'Fifteen Minutes of Fame' during their finest moments in exaggerated poses on Facebook. Most of the time as a selfie.

Like I said, I often wonder to what extent these kind of pictures represent *reality,* and why the need to be captured *unreal* arises, since untrained people who start to perform usually look like bad actors in old fashioned movies.

Why is it so difficult to stay relaxed, look into the lens quietly and continue with what you're doing? Why all these *duck faces,* that posed, theatrical pseudo sexy, pouting photography, which especially girls and young women use to recommend themselves?

Uncertainty? Dissatisfaction with reality? Or corresponding to an assumed expectation as a form of acquired *normal* behaviour, belonging to photography, dating from the days of long exposure times when it was necessary to be conscious of what was happening and pose for seconds?

I remember Andy Warhol with his friendly soft spoken voice telling the person he was talking to when I was photographing him: "Stop talking, he's making a picture", after which he shut up, stood straight and looked self assuredly into the camera.

Because of this *camera consciousness,* which makes you, as the photographer, influence a situation merely by your presence, reality is manipulated at the moment you enter a room with only the idea of making a picture. Even before you unpack your camera or give any directions, you're already manipulating reality.

Of course, you – the photographer – decide when the shutter will be released, what story you want to tell but through interaction with the subject, you become 'visible' as well.

Unavoidable.

That's why I think it's rather unwise to behave very conspicuously or put yourself in the foreground when you're planning to bring out the specific strength and character of the people you photograph most effectively. Don't try to push your ideas about expression and emotion upon someone by means of loud and bragging direction, something I've been told some of my colleagues make a habit of.

When you are too extrovert, giving the impression you have to prove yourself all the time, and not able to open up to the person you're photographing, a kind of photography will arise in which your own behaviour will be reflected in the person you're photographing, which will have an determining effect on your pictures. Think for instance of the ex-Vogue photographer Terry Richardson who went all the way concerning this and nowadays appears in his pictures in person.

Maybe only very inconspicuous, almost invisible photographers like Vivian Maier, Robert Frank or Brassaï have been able to make pictures of people without interacting as a reaction to their presence. This made it possible for them to really show something of the other and his behaviour - where in fact, albeit in a very different way from that described above - something of their character becomes visible as well.

But probably also – especially Maier and Brassaï – because they were comfortable in the places they were making their pictures. They knew how to behave in order not to stand out, and were hardly noticed. In this way nobody had second thoughts about them. This made them the best of them all. *'Window'* photographers avant la lettre.

I remember how much time American photographer Charles Gatewood spent looking for an invisible car. "An invisible photographer needs an invisible car!", was what he said.

In the end he bought an old, medium size, dirty yellowish standard type of Ford, which made him feel low profile, so the people he had to photograph would never have the idea that someone important had arrived at their front door, which could make them decide to show a special, maybe non-existent side of themselves.

If you closely study a person's posture and movements, you can often get an impression of their mood from as far as a hundred meters away. Even a silhouette can tell a lot about someone. Chin up or chin down, erect or slouched.

These things intrigue me and sparked my interest in physical expression, such as rhythmic gymnastics, ballet and dance. Body language.

Sometimes, attitude and expression tell a story more clearly than words; something that has always fascinated me and which I used a lot in my work because it adds more than anything to the expression of emotion.

Lively, spontaneous pictures of people in motion – images which sometimes look like simple snapshots but do have meaning and a sense of emotion – are usually far harder to make than those that are posed and directed, shot in a studio where everything is controlled and coincidence excluded.

Arms and legs, moving in all directions, have to be in the right place at the right time in order to create the impression of real human action rather than the mechanical moves of a motorized robot.

At the same time, the light, the clothes, the position in relation to the background, the facial expression and the glance in the eyes – the *feel* – must be right, without being frozen and controlled. The contrast between fore- and background must be watched closely to avoid things blending into each other, while at the same time, ensuring that no trees, lampposts, church steeples, sky scrapers, indoor plants or flagpoles stick out of heads or other body parts of the people you photograph, because that looks silly. You might get the impression they're wearing a funny hat or have a banner sticking out of their behind.

In other words, you must be able to push the button at the right moment to a much higher degree than when making static pictures.

In the end such a *moving* picture will look effortless, as if it's made without any craftsmanship or endeavor and will, ironically, be judged by a shallow reasoning spectator as a snapshot, easy to make. Further, when looking at a posed, constructed picture, it's usually easy to see how much thought and energy have been put in to it to achieve the final result.

During fashion shoots I used to make pictures of the surroundings where *the story* took place, e.g. without models, quickly in between shots, when the models were changing clothes or being treated by the make-up artist. Moreover, when I wasn't working I often photographed *cityscapes* in order to find out what possibilities they offered as backgrounds for future fashion shoots. Doors, walls, streets, squares, bridges, parks and so on. Pictures that someday might serve as a back-ground or as an idea for a new series. I kept these images in an archive. As a reminder, for *you never know.*

The environment where you make your pictures has a lot of impact on the atmosphere of the story you want to tell, and has an inspiring influence.

Sometimes these *location* pictures were used to add more context or as illustration to deepen the story.

Abstract compositions of shape and colour, form without content. As always, I was, only concerned with the way things looked in the picture, not what they really were. Only the *feel* of the subject was important to me. Old and aged, dilapidated, modern or futuristic, idyllic, rustic and so on.

Where buildings were concerned, I usually only showed a detail or a small part, hardly ever a building in its totality. Backgrounds were meant as an indication of atmosphere and circumstances, human emotion always came first.

Only when there was a direct connection between the building and the depicted person - think of a member of the boards or an employee – I would put them pontifically in front of a building, or maybe in case I wanted to *dwarf* someone, portraying a person small and unimportant. Usually I concentrated on the person and showed the building indistinctly in the background.

4. Staging and Directing

Staging and fiction – fully accepted in film, literature and painting - has long been considered as something negative in photography, as if photography should be limited to documentary – the depiction of reality - and that the expression of a personal vision or fantasy belonged to other disciplines.

Until ten years ago it was possible to hear a photo critic say: "That's a good picture, *but* it's not real."

I always asked myself what that actually meant, *real* in a picture.

As we have seen earlier, a photograph is never *real* or *true*. but always an interpretation of reality; a personal vision, acquired by means of technique, by definition subjective.

You choose a lens with a certain focal distance, an angle to shoot from, a frame within which a selected part of reality will be depicted. A decision must be made about what will happen in fore- or background and if you are going to use colour or black and white, to which we are accustomed but which in fact adds an abstract touch.

The next thing if you don't want to use flash, HMI or tungsten is waiting for the sun.

This can all be influenced by the use of various kinds of filters or close-up lenses to add extra subjective effects and then, finally, at *the decisive moment*, the shutter can be released.

But there's more.

If you haven't already used completely accepted, 'old fashioned' darkroom techniques like pushing or modulating – techniques that are making a comeback – you can start up a raster graphics editing program such as, for some still controversial, *Photoshop*.

One way or the other, we are always dealing with a personal vision of 'reality' which makes what you see in a photograph never 'real', but always subjective.

Or, as Richard Avedon once said: "All photographs are accurate. None of them is the truth."

Which of course is no problem at all. As John Szarkowski already showed us, a picture is in the first place about what something looks like in the image, not about what it is.

What it really is, the famous Dutch photo-detective Hans Aarsman can tell us. His more specific observations can give you an opinion which differs from previously-held views. He can even provide a new and different insight.

However my experience has taught me what my sub-consciousness already knew, long before I found a magnifying glass; namely, that while observing pictures, primary and secondary emotions are usually similar.

Maybe that's personal because in case, for example I found a light blue sports bag, not my own, lying on my hotel room bed - something that happened to the detective – I would understand that I had ended up in the wrong room, while the detective does not make this connection right away and takes for granted that this reaction is applicable to everyone.

If a picture *looks* as if it's made spontaneously, uncontrived, straight from the heart, it will *look* real, and that's what pictures are about. That's enough. It doesn't necessarily *have* to be made spontaneously, uncontrived, straight from the heart. Further considerations are rational and don't apply to emotional values.

As with the extremely touching, world famous, 1994 *Pulitzer prize* winning picture of *The Vulture and the Little Girl* by Kevin Cartner, a picture in which it seems as though a toddler is going to be attacked by a vulture. In spite of a rational explanation which exonerated the photographer of the accusation of not having intervened, the critics kept on blaming him, until he decided to take his own life due to depression a couple of months later.

The child, which turned out to be a boy, lived to be seventeen, and the place where he found himself in the picture was frequented by vultures all the time, it being a feeding center where they were waiting for leftovers.

It was no use.

It didn't change the emotions the picture evoked.

It is quite easy to photograph things and situations in a way that makes visual content deceptive or ambiguous, by lighting, point of view, angle, you name it.

Then the photo detective can say what he likes but the picture doesn't give the impression you are looking at what is photographed and will usually be considered less than good, or, at best, very *creative*. The picture doesn't work as a means of communication, we only *know* the picture is about something other than what we see.

Bad photography.

Since we're making more pictures than ever and we - photographers as well as amateurs - are all used to digital manipulation, it doesn't seem to make any difference anymore whether something is real or not.

It looks as though this new awareness has made us run on to the other side and that real and unreal don't exist at all anymore. Mise-en-scene as well as digital manipulation, 'anything goes', are generally accepted nowadays as a form of self expression, while photographers who are working in this field have started to call themselves artists.

This is nothing new however, because mise-en-scene and direction have actually always been used in photography right from the beginning, usually invisible.

Think for instance of the world famous *spontaneous* picture by Doisneau who in Paris, while shooting *The Kiss*, instructed his models from a terrace and must have said something like "Embrasse! Maintenant!", or of David Bailey with his subtle "Smile with your eyes" or Dutch photographer Ed van der Elsken, who asked the Teddy boys in Amsterdam to look at least a little tough! It is commonly known that Cartier-Bresson asked the old lady on *Cape Cod* to hold a U.S. flag, while Eisenstadt admitted to having screamed something like "Grab that chick!" when he saw *something white* flashing during the *V-J Day* celebrations on *Times Square*.

Like a father directing his daughter while photographing her on the beach: "C'mon love, smile!"

And why not? Even if Rosenthal actually staged his Iwo Jima picture, so what? They were fighting there and that flag had to be planted somewhere anyway.

When I heard that Diane Arbus, when making her famous picture of *the boy with the hand grenade*, circled around him long enough to be able to capture the "Fuck-off-bitch-leave-me-alone-you're-driving-me-nuts" look in his eyes, I understood that this was an artistically driven action. For a spectator, this is a completely invisible kind of direction to obtain a better picture.

Arbus manipulated reality in one of her most iconic pictures. The realization that I had always been on the wrong track about this, in thinking all of her pictures were uncontrived representation of reality, was an extraordinary experience. I was completely astounded!

However, the picture doesn't lose its strength and stays credible because when looking at it you don't realize the image is actually *staged* and what you feel is what counts in a photograph, not what it actually is that you're looking at or how it came about.

The important thing is that someone else can see what *you* think and feel, that you show what *you* see. Whether it be staged or not, doesn't matter. But, as we have seen before, if you realize at first impression that it's not a confronting picture you're looking at but a picture made to confront - that the emotion is artificial and contrived – you'll realize you're looking at kitsch which for that reason, will, in spite of all kinds of new developments and visions, only appeal to a small audience.

Just as it always happens when making portraits – chin up, head a little to the left – when shooting documentary it feels quite natural to interfere with reality through physical directions; sometimes to create a *more realistic* reality than reality itself. All in order to achieve a communicatively seen, *better* result, which, no question, is pure manipulation; completely understandable, and fully accepted, but manipulation it is.

Another form of manipulation from the one Diane Arbus used when making the picture of the boy with the hand grenade, is what Arnold Newman did when shooting his famous portrait of Stravinsky, a picture that decorated one of the walls of my studio for more than 25 years without ever having bored me.

He created a fabulous image by watching closely through his viewfinder, balancing frame and composition in such a way that form and content influence each other making both of them become stronger.

Looking at Newman's pictures it sometimes seems that the people portrayed don't even realize they're being photographed. They are part of an image that looks as if it's made without them knowing they're in it. A little to the back with the camera, a bit to the right, figure in the corner! And click! "Got it!"

In my opinion, working this way Newman is more of a photographer than Arbus. Whereas Arbus concentrates on anthropology and chooses for the simplest form – square format, belly perspective, subject in the middle – which takes care of a direct confrontation with the content of the image – Newman combines form and content, and intensifies and emphasizes content by form. The composition is clearly visible. Beautiful but visibly craving effect.

Looking at the work of a photographer like Vivian Maier, everything looks as if it came into place organically – definitely uncontrived, credible; natural rather than posed. Maier wins. Her pictures are among the best work I know.

If I had discovered her work sooner she could have been a lifelong influence for me. Sadly, this was impossible because she didn't publish one picture during her lifetime and her archives were found only recently.

Now it was the other *master of spontaneity* Jacques Henri – "Throw that dog over the ditch!" – Lartigue.

Could've been worse.

Without exception all of my fashion pictures are staged. However, they were never completely planned, 'designed' in advance, but fitted into a wider concept and were based on an idea or an emotion, an image of time, a movie, a novel, a philosophy, mutual understanding etcetera. That became the story. The *theme* if you will.

With that idea in mind I made sketches that were used as a starting point but were never meant to be executed literally. Personally I always found it hard to commit myself to rules and concepts figured out in advance to achieve good results. During a shoot, things would often look different from what

I'd imagined. Sometimes I had to change my mind every hour, depending on the weather or other unpredictable circumstances, so you have to be flexible and open to coincidence; sometimes just in order to save time, but also because there's a chance that you come across things that are visually more interesting and could not have been predicted at any point.

Serendipity.

Due to this flexibility and as a result of unforeseen occurrences on location, so to speak, when I and the crew of models, stylists and make-up artists, joined 'real life' and like a street photographer, went out onto the streets, my results sometimes differed from my preconceptions.

It was in this way that my desired *new reality* came into being, with humanity as context, a context that can be understood by anyone, including those who are not interested in fashion.

Despite a lot of styling and make-up, these shoots reached a certain level of reality because the models didn't pose but *became people* by showing emotions and feelings and maybe something of their character or personality, which I, somewhere between portrait- and documentary photography, only had to capture: Constructed Realism.

While shooting in Italy, working on *Una Donna Particolare,* there was one thing of which the stylist and I were absolutely certain: we were going to photograph our model sitting on the back of a bike with a priest.

She ended up with a farmer. On a donkey cart.

The possibility of being able to make use of unexpected circumstances is one of the most intriguing sides of this profession. As a result of this, however, a client never knows in advance what the final result will look like.

This means there needs to be trust and adaptability to provide someone who works the way I do with a budget to go on a trip with at least a handful of people and pay for all expenses.

Working for magazines this will happen sooner than for commercial assignments because magazine productions are usually the result of cooperation between photographer and stylist-producer - often the same person - without explicit interference from an editorial staff or art-director beforehand.

Magazines don't have endless meetings with clients, members of the board of directors, and other interested parties to discuss the desired concepts and strategies which are customary working practices for advertising agencies.

Usually a short, verbal instruction is all: "Think summer!" or "Passion!"

Commercial clients, on the other hand, expect clear agreements and ultimately want to see exactly what is agreed upon. They, understandably, want 'value' for their money. That's the deal.

Once, I had to go to a city with a southern, Mediterranean feel to photograph an advertising campaign, of which, apart from a lot of traffic and palm trees, a blue sky was part of the concept. We didn't make any pictures because – just like in Nice and in Rome, where we went successively - it was overcast.

If I had made pictures – which I would have done for a magazine – I wouldn't have stuck with the concept and by doing so, badly executed my assignment.

Because I hadn't made the intended images, the client would - I'm pretty sure about that - not have been satisfied which means I would probably have lost him as a commissioner, but because the campaign *had* to be shot - advertising space was already reserved – the whole crew would have had to go on another trip, and they would probably have booked another photographer.

Now I was booked to try it for a third time.

This time successfully.

Pheww!

As I said before, when working with models I think it's important to depict them as *people* and not as *models*.

I never liked model-like poses with arms *akimbo* and a sniffy look, not to mention pouting or a hand touching a slightly opened mouth. Unless they had to look like a posing model of course.

The opposite, making pictures of people, posing like models in overacted, unnatural ways is as old as photography itself, and became a habit accepted by many.

Think for instance of the kitschy, posed pictures that the English photographer Jimmy Nelson made for his book *Before They Pass Away.* It's easy to imagine the jeans and i-phones of the people portrayed, hidden in the bushes, out of frame but still he received the *Anna Cornelis Public Prize* for it.

Despite a large amount of fans, there were many people – especially representatives of the depicted people themselves – who didn't like the title and the unnatural way the people were photographed or felt abused by Nelson because of his financial intentions.

The photographer defended himself by saying he wanted to photograph them by "putting them in the context of international top model Kate Moss", which caused him to be criticized by the people who dislike the glamour world of Kate Moss.

My idea would be to show Kate Moss as well as the primitive people of Jimmy Nelson in their own context.

In that case the pictures themselves take care of the stories they're telling and it would not be necessary to provide them with a book full of enhanced stories.

Usually, however, this frequently encountered, gaudy way of posing is part of a fashion shoot with the idea of directing attention to the clothes; a kind of photography we know from the past, practiced by photographers such as Edward Steichen, Cecil Beaton, Hoyningen-Huene or Horst P. Horst, who left an indelible and unparalleled impression with their dramatically lit fashion pictures, usually shot in a studio, and dating from the first half of the twentieth century. Pictures that, regardless of their enormous expressive strength, now – for they reflect their time - look outdated.

These somewhat fictitious, *contrived* pictures became a reality in themselves, with meaning and importance for those who are interested in fashion and celebrities.

It is probably the watered down, pale shadow of this genre of posed, unnatural, but to this day still imitated fashion pictures that is responsible for the negative image of shallowness and stupidity of fashion photography in general that exists for many people.

Maybe it's a good idea to look at the photographs of Peter Lindbergh or Arthur Elgort for a change, to see some viable alternatives.

These days people don't seem to know better. As Madonna sang: "Strike a pose! Vogue, Vogue, Vogue!"

More interesting is the kind of fashion photography focused on the depicted persons themselves because of the emotion they evoke, the mood they're in, or because of the visible exceptional situation they're in. A realistic approach, close to what's actually happening. Models don't have to perform all kinds of gymnastics or act like they're engaged in something and look into the camera at the same time. They only have to show some emotion, which is not as easy as it sounds. Through that they will grab your attention, causing the spectator to identify with the subject and finally become interested in what is shown.

When a subject looks into the camera, makes *eye contact* with the viewer, the spectator becomes part of the staged scene which is the reason people in my pictures only seldom look into the lens, portraits and close-ups being the exception. It's an old principle from the art of painting and probably the reason my work is often called *filmic*. Just like in movies, my models are seemingly oblivious to the presence of a camera, the reason they look *real*.

Working in this way the viewer stays spectator, watcher of another reality.

Of course the absence of camera contact is a method of direction for the benefit of a concept made up in advance: realism. It is, however, invisible, the image looks *natural*.

When shooting portraits this is different because portraits are usually about the person photographed in the first place, whose mood, state of mind, and temper is primarily reflected in the eyes and the muscles around them. To capture that is, in my opinion, essential for a good portrait.

5. Portraits

It is quite possible that the first portraits ever were made thousands of years ago, using charcoal, mud, or blood on the walls of caves, where rugged looking people, dressed in animal skins, found their shelter.

This being the case, the making of portraits is probably as old as humanity itself. The oldest preserved portraits known to man, the *Fayum* portraits, date from the time of the Egyptians, so I presume all possibilities and approaches must surely have been considered by now, whereby the art of portraiture has over time gained its own rules and laws.

It appears, nevertheless, that many photographers are repeatedly trying to reinvent the wheel. It is in this way that, in the absence of historical knowledge and probably in their will to innovate and express themselves, century old laws are trampled upon.

I'm definitely not against experimentation and innovation and think you have to be open to changes and always have to look for new ways but not - because of a thirst for sensation or desire for self-affirmation - when this leads to corniness, waggishness, ugliness, distortion or the expression of false emotions.

Why do someone's ears catch light while the eyes, the most important, focal point in a person's face, remain in the dark? Why is a spotlight directed at someone's shoulder or cheek, which attracts attention to that part; or is a nose lit from both sides which a makes it look like a little sailing boat drawn by a child? Why does someone make a picture of a person lit by a light coming from so high that only the upper side of his skull and the tip of his nose, the so called *pigeon-landing*, catches any light?

I cannot imagine!

This kind of experimental lighting usually doesn't add anything to the depiction of the character of the subject.

I often see portraits in which the emotions are posed or acted out, fake. One acts as *if* one is afraid, angry, happy, sad, sexy, shy or pious.

Of course emotions can be acted, nothing wrong with that, but when you try to give the impression of depicting *the truth*, reality *as you see it* and tell something about the nature and character of the portrayed, you should at least not be aware that it is acted, unless of course, you want to depict someone consciously as an actor or a clown.

If it's obvious that the emotions are acted, the picture, and also the persons photographed, will lose all credibility - in my eyes one of the most important criteria when evaluating staged photography - and appear as bad actors and actresses in a cheap b-movie, or as clowns, purveyors of false emotions.

In my opinion, one of the most important things regarding portraits is that the subject at least be recognizable.

I often see 'portraits' featuring someone photographed from behind or with a hat drawn over the eyes, or wearing dark sunglasses. Artefacts such as hats, caps, glasses, you name it, can tell a lot about a person, but when present in such an intrusive way that the subject becomes unrecognizable to an outsider who might encounter him or her unawares, then the photo fails at something.

In portrait photography one often speaks about *the core*. "Back to the core", is what some photographers say or "Making the core visible", which of course makes no sense.

The *core* as such doesn't exist.

A human being is a complicated sum of characteristics, emotions and changing moods, many of which are reflected in their facial expression which, along with their physiognomy, make up a large part of their identity; in a picture, however, you can only see what the subject looks like at some point in time. That's all. You don't see *who* he is. There is no such a thing as a *visible* essence. Something of the character can be made visible through the glance in the eyes and facial expression, and you can call that an *authentic* or maybe *honest* portrait, but that's it, you'll never see the complete person.

A photographic portrait of a person, made a second before or after another portrait of the same person, but in a slightly different light or from a slightly different angle, can give us the impression we are dealing with someone completely different. Someone with a different character, in a different state of mind.

"Will the real person stand up?"

As a result of the interaction between the person portrayed and the photographer the pictures will show the mark of the photographer because this interaction is usually similar. It repeatedly happens like this, the style of the photographer, according to characteristic vision and direction. In this way, *recognizability* or familiarity arises, a personal style, in which the character of the photographer and their way of socializing with people is reflected. If they always employ the same technique, one will immediately be able to recognize their work.

In this way a portrait can tell us more about the creator than about the subject, or as Richard Avedon once said "My portraits are more about me than they are about the people I photograph." - as Oscar Wilde remarked before him: "Every portrait that is painted with feeling is a portrait of the artist, not of the sitter."

Such words are often quoted and used as a device for focusing attention on the maker rather than on the person portrayed. Consequently people are used merely as an object, an easy road to self expression.

A rare exception was the *invisible* English photographer Jane Bown, who recently died, age 89. For over 50 years she made portraits of 'the rich and famous, the infamous and unknown' for the Observer, a British Sunday broadsheet. She photographed people like Beckett, Hockney, Lennon, Nurejev, Björk, Cocteau, Welles and Hopper, you name it, even Richard Nixon and the Queen of England, all in black and white and on location; no special lights, no tricks, no fakery, just a simple camera; always catching the right moment, giving the impression you're looking at the person photographed and not at yet another self-portrait of the photographer. Jane Bown: "The best pictures come from the unforeseen. They suddenly appear out of nowhere. One moment they are there, the next they are gone. It is very simple to take a picture, but it is very difficult to make a good photograph."

It's clear that a good portrait shows both the subject and the creator, despite the fact that not everybody shares the same opinion on this. Some photographers consider their portraits, for instance, as *reflections of social sentiments* - as Dutch photographer Rineke Dijkstra does – or their personal *coming of age problemacy*, visions in which the people portrayed act more or less as objects, tools that help to achieve the artistic goals of the creator.

In my opinion a portrait is about the subject, and not the photographer and their irresistible urge towards self expression, their umpteenth self portrait.

Even when the techniques employed are simple, the subjective vision of the photographer is inevitable and will give a portrait its signature, unless the creator is a impersonal *photo machine* that merely records, leaving all direction in the hands of the person who is being photographed,

It's remarkable that many internationally-acclaimed photographers rely mainly on traditional portrait techniques (in e.g. lighting, framing and pose) and are not constantly trying to improve their work by means of spectacular technical stunts which usually involve only form.

Think for instance of Avedon, Bailey, Knight, Leibovitch or Penn. They usually work with only one light source, and usually use *Rembrandt-* or *Butterfly lighting*, often frontal, originating just a little higher than the camera's point of view; sometimes – immediately adding lots of contrast – from one side, like Belgian photographer Stephan Vanfleteren.

Dutch *pop* photographer and filmmaker Anton Corbijn is an exception. He makes his celebrity portraits mainly with available natural light, which is much more difficult than it would seem, due to the limited capacity for control.

It is not necessary to come up with something new or innovative to make a good studio portrait. An effective atmosphere can still be achieved by simply using just one light source, paying attention to detail and giving a certain amount of direction, e.g. head a little up or down, turning to left or right. Factors such as these can make a big difference.

Reflection screens to brighten shadows should only be used with great care and never from a low angle – unless you want to make the portrayed person look like a ghost; also not from the side, as this will work as a second light source, which causes the face to become darker towards the back and then suddenly light again - very distorting and quite unnatural.

In the pictures by the photographers mentioned above I rarely see the use of fill-in or backlight, not to mention the notorious light from both sides, a little from behind, where two light sources of the same intensity are used on both sides of the face, producing a visibly fictitious, artificial, mutilating effect, i.e. a very unnatural, distorting kind of lighting that immediately puts the sitter in a *fraught* light. Think of Arnold Newman's portrait of Alfried Krupp.

Some photographers consider the light they're using as their signature, regardless of what a person looks like. I personally think it's your vision that counts, the light you use possibly being helpful; and that you should aim for a good portrait, and not for the acknowledgement of a special technique. My advice is to keep the light simple, if possible rich in contrast, whilst concentrating on the relation with the subject. Make sure the person you photograph really looks like and radiates what *you* want him to look like or radiate. It's all about *your* view of the person, that's all.

In my experience, and when I look at some of the strongest portraits I know, shot by for instance Richard Avedon or Annie Leibovitch, it is the simply-lit photographs, with all emphasis on the subject, that get the best results.

To be able to build up a confidential relationship with someone within a short time - whereby you can make people feel at ease, so they can be themselves - is part of a photographer's craftsmanship. This component should not be under-estimated, especially when making portraits on commission, because those photographs are not the product of an emotional relationship but made as an assignment.

While making pictures on commission, when contact with the sitter is usually of short duration and superficial in nature, the possibility can arise that you make portraits that end up feeling forced, causing you to make pictures *of* people instead of *about* people. It is important, therefore, to take your time, put the person at ease or drive him to madness, whichever you prefer, and CLICK!

Probably as a reaction to the digitally-slickened glamour images we regularly see nowadays - which make us long for a return to *authenticity* - we've seen the reintroduction of a technique I mentioned previously: the wet plate collodion process, a laborious form of photography whereby, using big wooden bellows cameras and mostly antique lenses, positives are directly shot on plates on a layer of glass or metal.

Just like *Polaroids*, unique editions, one by one.

Because of the specific chromatic sensitivity of these *wet plates,* the characteristic development stains and smudges and the use of mostly original, towards the borders soft toning lenses, an image appears which is typical of the social-status-affirming pictures dating from the second half of the nineteenth century.

Because of the limited sensitivity of the plates, it's not possible to make snapshots using this technique because the subject has to sit still for several seconds, which results in a 'silencing' in the eyes and the facial muscles. During these long exposure times, the head is kept in place by using a kind of a clamp attached to the chair and the neck of the subject.

"A sense of peace and quiet and distinction is what makes these images so special", is what fans of these static, serious pictures will say.

A spontaneous moment, however, a genuine smile or an incidental glance, is something you'll never see. No *decisive* moment. Gone. Something I regret, because many techniques that have developed over the years are left unused, and with it, the ability to depict some of the volatility of life is totally neglected; so also the potential to depict unique, one-off moments and register brief emotions - in my opinion one of the most outstanding and distinctive characteristics of modern photography.

By using of this antique process, a welcome achievement in arriving at a more realistic and expressive image is thrown overboard on behalf of a form that can't depict spontaneity.

Because of possible motion blur, this results in everybody, regardless of personal demeanour, looking like a more or less serious person.

Furthermore, wasn't it Martin Parr, one of world's most influential and highly classified photographers, who once said: "Who in their right mind would want to lock themselves away and play with chemicals, when today an inkjet printer can render a print of quality equal to that of a traditional analogue print and of superior archival durability?"

Or words to that effect.

The first impression I get when looking at a wet plate portrait is that I'm looking at a picture that was made about hundred years ago and that the depicted person has undoubtedly since passed away. This is caused by my historical esthetical awareness which has become part of my consciousness over the years; let's call it the *nostalgic* effect.

Subsequently I'm surprised when I discover that I'm familiar with the portrayed person and recently talked to him on the telephone and that I read one of his Facebook posts a few hours ago. To top it all, he's wearing contemporary clothing!

Confusing, you might say. Something is wrong. The person I see in the photograph is emotionally dead yet simultaneously alive. Probably a zombie.

In a similar vein, it's noteworthy that when I hear reactions to this kind of photography, people often refer to persons or photographers who died a long time ago. "Isn't that Shostakovich!", or "Hey, Hemmingway!", "Kafka", "Wow, is this an unknown August Sander?" or "Oh oh, Dracula!"

It is clear that the images are putting many spectators on the wrong track. Regarding photography this is nothing new in itself, but usually this happens because of *the lie*, the vision of the photographer. However, this time the confusion arises because of the form, and not because of the content, which is essentially different.

Clearly, something is visibly wrong. The portrayed person is dead and alive at the same time.

As I have said, in my opinion portrait photography is about showing something of the personality of the depicted person, as seen by the photographer.

Readers will not be surprised to hear about my hesitation to be photographed by someone using wet plate collodion photography. Brr.

Recently some American magazines and newspapers published articles about Victoria Will, a young American photographer who shot many portraits using this process, *Tin Plate Portraits*. At the same time, the technique was subject to widespread experimentation. Most people who try this use antique *Petzval* lenses, make their own plates – usually aluminum covered with a light sensitive layer – and prepare their own chemicals.

All of these pictures, mainly portraits, have the same sepia hue, characteristic *in focus - out of focus* effect and usually plenty of stains.

The difference between the work of Will and many of her colleagues is that she photographed contemporary celebrities - Philip Seymour Hoffman, not long before he died, Kurt Russel, Anne Hathaway, Kristen Stewart, Maggie Gyllenhaal, Nick Cave and so on, while many others - despite all kinds of fantasies about flying people and photo-producing type writers - stuck to portraits of their beloved, their colleagues and other acquaintances.

Most of these pictures are usually quite strong but dreary, fire our imagination and look as if they originated in the distant past.

In my opinion, however, these photographs would impress us more if they showed artists or celebrities, as in Will's pictures, whilst now, most people will wonder who all these people actually are. You get used to the old fashioned effect quite quickly, especially when you see a great many of them together, so in the end you're just looking at repeats, who usually show little emotion because of the long exposure times. Because of this, these portraits are not as strong and lively as they might be.

I suppose, despite the exceptional quality of these works, it will mainly be the subjects themselves, their best friends and maybe a few members of their families, who are going to be interested in an exposition or publication of these pictures.

The fact that there are two or three people who are known by the public will not change this. It's comforting to look at pictures of people you admire amidst the enormous number of images the media cause you to consume on a daily basis. Like a material confirmation of an emotional tie. The idea that someone you love or long for is near, despite his or her absence.

People love to look at celebrities as a means of emotional support. Photographing the rich and famous is the key to success for many photographers; as in the old days for Nadar who photographed most of the Parisian artistic and intellectual elite in the mid nineteenth century. It's clear that with this kind of photography the pictures are first and foremost about the portrayed people themselves and less about the vision of the photographer.

In interviews with celebrity photographers, it is usual to pay more attention to the celebrities themselves than to the specific qualities of the photographer. Even when the photographer is outstanding.

"If you want to become famous, you have to photograph famous people!" is what Paul Huf, a renowned Dutch photographer used to say.

And that is what he did.

We have seen that a profound interest in the subject, in this case the people you photograph, is more important than the technique you're using. After all it's something of the character, the personality or human dignity, of the person you photograph that you're trying to show. Therein lies the real importance of a portrait, which has little to do with the chosen form. Special cameras and lenses, extraordinary filters or effects influence the form but can only incidentally contribute to vision; while it is vision that shows the specific qualities of a photographer and, because it's personal, the only way to distinguish one photographer from another.

Form can support vision but form without vision only shows technical ability and can be learned and adjusted by anyone.

The short movie about the American photographer Dennis Manarchy *Butterflies and Buffalo: Tales of American Culture* shows how he builds an enormous 35 foot camera, capable of producing massive prints in pristine high-pixel clarity. Manarchy, once an assistant of Irving Penn, shoots 4.5 x 6 foot film negatives, producing images with over 1000 times more visual detail than today's most advanced digital cameras. This was something hitherto unseen in photography, creating the possibility to make prints of, sometimes, two stories high.

With this gigantic camera, the size of a semi-trailer, he travels the United States to depict fifty different cultures. He had made many portraits before, using smaller cameras but he was never really satisfied with the results. Now he likes what he sees in the final prints, and he's convinced that it's all down to his camera.

When I compare the early photographs to the ones he's making now, I barely see any difference. What does strike me, however, is how decent, honest and sensible his portraits are. When I see him working in his studio or hear him talk about the people he's photographing, the first thing I notice is his love and commitment regarding his subjects.

He wants so much to show others how special he thinks all these people are, how fascinated he is by them, that he was not only willing, but thought it was absolutely essential to build this gigantic camera. He is convinced that thanks to this camera and the complicated darkroom activities his pictures are better. I think it is the result of his enormous engagement and love for his subjects which makes his new work so outstanding, something he doesn't fully realize because it is part of his character. For Manarchy it's absolutely normal and self-evident one is interested in these people.

6. Fashion and Trends

Fashion is a deeply rooted social-cultural phenomenon in which, according to often unspoken codes and agreements, conscious or not, people show their inner self to the world. It can therefore be considered as part of their identity.

Fashion not only refers to style of dress, hair and make-up but also includes music, language, art, cuisine, architecture and even the thinking, popular in a culture at any given time. Omnipresent, constantly changing. The Zeitgeist.

It is simplistic to consider fashion as *shallow*. Even an aversion to fashion is a reaction, an involuntary engagement. Or as Coco Chanel once said: "Fashion is not something that exists in dresses only. Fashion is in the sky, in the street, fashion has to do with ideas, the way we live and what is happening."

There is no actual proof but it is very likely that the first human beings already felt the urge to express and distinguish themselves from one another by means of accessories and decoration, behaviour still found in some remote parts of the world – one or two bones sticking through their noses, animal skins with or without the tail, hat feathers, worn either singly or in a bunch.

Nowadays there are groups of people who try to express their individuality by means of common life-style choices. They prepare vegetarian dishes whilst wearing hand-knitted sweaters and discuss the creation of their vegetable gardens in their own idiom. While enjoying a glass of organic wine, sitting on Arne Jacobsen chairs, they're deceived by the illusion that they're different from everyone else.

Throughout history, and all over the world, in all cultures, the significance of fashion as a distinguishing feature, is commonly found. It is a form of primal behavior, interrelated with the human condition and not just a side effect of modern economic standards. It is also the reason why fashion photography is more than just making pictures of dresses; a kind of photography considered by some of the world's most influential and highly valued photographers as their primary means of self-expression.

Some of them even made their best and most famous work in this field. Think for instance of Avedon, Bailey, Beaton, Blumenfeld, Bourdin, Elgort, Horst, Klein, Lindbergh, Meisel, Newton, Penn, Sacha, Sherman, Shore, Sieff, Sorrenti, Steichen, Stern, Teller, Testino, Toscani, Van de Wijngaard, Van Lamsweerde - Matadin, Von Unwerth or Weber.

All masters of their profession, craftsmen in addition to being proficient in fashion, often comfortable with various disciplines; from portrait and documentary to landscape and architecture.

Despite current changes– with recent expositions of Bailey, Beaton, and Horst in London, and Blumenfeld, Bourdin, and Newton in Berlin and Paris – fashion photography has long been considered a poor relation and seen as less important than social, documentary or *art* photography. "Fashion is shallow, superficial. Not important.", is something you still hear some critics say. "No need to pay attention to it."

But, just as with photography itself, the appreciation of fashion photography - here we go again - is subject to fashion.

In some countries one starts to realize that this kind of photography can be a valuable cultural expression, according to some *belonging in the pantheon of art history.*

Because of this, fashion photography has entered the museums of modern art where it can now be found not only exhibited in the basements but in the upper galleries as well. The fact that international day-rates of top-fashion photographers are considered to be the highest in the field – think in terms of 100.000 to 150.000 dollars a day – indicates that something more complicated than just registering the latest summer fashion is going on. Something that probably has to do with a combination of craftsmanship, sense of aesthetics and ability to visualize the Zeitgeist. Knowing and sensing what's going on in the world.

For me, fashion photography has always been a way to integrate my imagination into reality in order to create and record a new, temporary reality. Something inherent to my fascination for the human condition in general and more specifically, for youth culture, film, painting and music.
I have never wished to register just a trend or fashion, but have always tried to create a timeless, universal view of the human condition in relation to the times we are living in. The more realistically this was done, the more believable it would appear in the picture.

On a quest for that timeless, universal human image, I always tried to avoid the ever changing trends to which fashion photography is in itself subject. Despite the fact that I have never been able to restrain from this often unrealistic approach completely - typical fashion -, I always attempted to integrate fashion into fictional, dramatized, but realistic situations. I did this without the use of typical photographic tools such as extreme tele- or wide angle lenses, colour filters, constructed lighting or deviant ways of printing etc. Such techniques are mainly about form, aiming for effect, and have no significance whatsoever where content is concerned. They only create a sense of alienation. For the same reason I prefer lenses with normal focal distances, available light rather than artificial light, existing locations over studio decors, and acting and naturally moving models over posing ones. I hardly ever use photographical applications such as special developing or printing techniques because they, just like the afore-mentioned lenses and filters, are mainly about form and stimulate the alienation of a realistic content.

By working in this way, the mix of reality and fiction I was looking for simply evolved, along with the desired image. It minimized the possibility for the pictures to look contrived and affected, fake, like situations created merely for the occasion of the shoot.

Looking for that timeless, human image in which the person photographed plays the central part, and not the outfit that he or she is wearing, I always, deliberately, tried to avoid anything *trendy*. I have never been able to become particularly excited about the *latest fashion* because I realize there is a strong chance it will be *passé* by tomorrow. It's the human element that attracts me in photography, the clothes people are wearing come in second place.

I have always found this approach to be more interesting and important than photographing a style or trend simply because it was fashionable at the time. This has occasionally been criticized by some of my clients. They expected it to be clear when exactly a picture was shot, which was not always the case. The irony was that, from my perspective of timelessness and universality, I usually took their criticism as a compliment!

Now, fifteen years later, with considerable distance and a changed street view - looking at styles in clothing, hair and make-up, the lack of mobile phones, for instance - it is clear that most of my work is shot during the last part of the second half of the twentieth century. The exact month and year, people may figure that out for themselves.

7. Art and Craftsmanship

As a photographer you have to be confident. Your work will be judged by spectators with different visions.

If you let this influence you, you will soon become confused, because the opinions of professionals, amateurs, and art critics can differ greatly.

Professionals know how a picture is made. They master the techniques necessary to depict an idea, their own as well as those of others. They can make a picture suitable for its intended use and make a living from it.

They look at a photograph differently from a non-professional, someone who has only made an occasional holiday picture or a selfie, and usually considers a photograph as a representation of reality, a fact: "The camera doesn't lie! That's the way it was!"

Art critics look at the art-historical perspective of a photograph and determine whether or not it fits into the local or international trends of a widely-renowned gallery or museum, regardless of their personal preferences.

More and more people buy art as an investment, making it an international currency, uncontrolled by any member of the *International Organization of Securities Commissions.* Art is not only collected because of its emotional values or because it fits within a collection. Many collectors consider their purchases as investments. There is also a sense of prestige associated with paying large amounts of money for a piece of art. The value of art, however, is only consistent if collectors listen to each other, and friends and acquaintances also buy art by the same artist. In this way a market is created, enabling some photographers to become more famous by the day. If you want a great photograph hanging on your wall their name will ensure that it is of high quality and has rigidity of value. No knowledge of photography is needed for that. The importance of an artist is mainly determined by how much money they earn. Craftsmanship has very little to do with it. In ten, fifteen years, when a new generation arrives and new artists are on trend, everything will be different. Business as usual.

It is nevertheless the case that the art-establishment looks down somewhat disdainfully on commercial or publicity photography and it is often considered as a lesser form than photography by *artists*: "Money is SO vulgar, darling!" Commercial photography - which to many critics includes *shallow* fashion photography – is usually established very professionally and can be very spectacular, direct and self explanatory at the same time, making separate context-containing booklets redundant. Think for instance of the famous *Charles Jourdan* advertising campaign shot for years by Guy Bourdin.

Aficionados may speak with great aplomb of an 'art photograph' that is sold at an New York auction for, e.g. 30.000 US Dollars, but when a commercial photographer receives twice as much for an advertising picture, the noses stay firmly in the air!

Concepts and techniques used are often comparable. The only clear, apparent difference is that a commercial picture is used to sell something, while art photographs are themselves the commodity.

It is, of course, special when something hanging on a wall in a museum raises questions. When the most relevant question is "What's so special about this?" I'll start to wonder.

I once saw a documentary about the Dutch photographer Rineke Dijkstra famous for her beach pictures, photographs of adolescents in bathing suits on beaches.

Clearly visible for a professional, she was messing around with her 4x5 inch view camera. After having focused, for instance, she forgot to secure the rear standard which holds the ground glass; subsequently she had to search for the required button. Because of this it took quite some time to make an exposure, which caused the teenagers she was photographing to get bored and look at her with an expression like "Aren't you done yet? Tick-Tock.", and with matching postures.

Later, art-critics would say: "Do you see that? Isn't it fantastic? So typically of today's youth, that weak, insecure attitude, that apathetic look on their faces! Testament to the great vision of this artist!"

In an interview, many years later, the photographer - world famous by now with her zeitgeist representing, seemingly unemotional portraits – affirmed the opinion of the critics. "That was exactly the idea." she said. "By making these pictures extremely slowly, like a non professional, I wanted to make the teenagers stop thinking about what they wanted to look like, forget about their self image, in order to provoke them looking expressionless, apathetic, bored which was what I wanted to capture. That took some time."

An exceptional kind of direction which would make the adolescents on the beach look uncertain and disaffected. In an interview with the teenagers, however, you could see how interested and excited they were about the photo shoot which was planned for the following day, how positive they were about the idea of being photographed. They wanted to look cheerful and pretty in the photographs, the reason one of the girls even bought a new, orange bathing suit, however the photographer used the teenagers to give shape to a concept figured out in advance; in this case the preconceived idea that these children are characterless adolescents without a confident self image, tormented by uncertainty. This can only mean that these pictures are staged with the idea of selling something – very comparable with advertising photography. No bathing suits this time, however, but the social, critical and psychological ideas of the photographer.

At the same time we see again clearly that a photographic portrait is a personal, subjective vision which usually tells us more about the creator than about the person portrayed. In this case the portrayed persons become almost 'invisible' , because they are used merely as objects to convey a preconceived idea in order to achieve a personal artistic goal.

The idea behind the portraits – "we're living in a very demanding age in which expectations are hard to live up to, therefore we become uncertain and vulnerable, which we, fearing to be criticized, are trying to hide" – is universal and recognizable for many of us; something we all can clearly imagine. Because the photographer repeats her message with every new series, the idea builds confidence with the art loving public which makes her pictures very popular. "The best photographer of the Netherlands", I heard someone say at the opening of the renovated *Stedelijk Museum* in Amsterdam, where a separate gallery is devoted to the photographer of the beach pictures.

Was this because of her fill- in flash, bored, straight forward portraits which mainly reveal something about the photographer and ourselves? Or did we end up in a vicious circle where the fact that a museum gallery is named after her has become her chief qualification?

The constant repetition would certainly be most

unimpressive for a commercial photographer.

Sometimes it appears to me that her initial clumsy behaviour, having been so well-received by the critics, has become a kind of a trick, a device which causes people inadvertently to reveal their vulnerability: *the concept*. As such, it is at best unreliable!

A well known writer, once photographed by her, recently told me that during the sitting, she wasn't allowed to laugh, move, frown, you name it. She was completely constrained from being herself, even had to remain motionless for a particularly long time.

According to the subject, a very dynamic, expressive personality, the results were not worth looking at.

But what would *you* do? If other people tell you your work is extraordinary, offer you exhibitions in museums and are willing to pay large amounts of money for your prints, would you say "No"?

When you're successful as a photographer, showered with praise, covered with glory, the danger is that you'll lose your critical faculties and start repeating yourself, which in turn leads you up a blind alley. So stay alert, be self-critical, don't be easily satisfied. As Edward Steichen once said. "Every ten years a man should give himself a good kick in the pants."

When a well known art-critic states on TV that art has come such a long way for us to be able to appreciate such pictures as those described above, is he referring to our progressive insight or to his own fatigue and need for respite, caused by the enormous amount of imagery we're daily confronted with? I believe the latter to be the case but that it's really not that important; as is the case with trends, this one will also come to an end. A new star with a totally different story is already born! As I have said, photography also has its fashions.

In art circles, one often boasts about trivia, things relating to photography that are very common, or even not worth mentioning for a professional, things like *fill-in-flash* or *post exposure*. It occurs to me, that this may be due to a lack of technical knowledge. You can assume that when one can clearly see that a photographer has thought about a picture in advance, as if he has *designed* the image; or when one can discuss the technique employed, or perhaps when a picture is made under – for a non professional – seemingly difficult circumstances, a judgment will often turn out to be positive. A special leaflet will tell you what's so unique about the photograph you're looking at, and you'll probably find an explanation about the technical skills that are used.

It may be that the photographer has used a special camera, lens or computer program or exposed his pictures in moonlight. This doesn't impress a professional. In my eyes the true art is to ignore technique, not allowing it to count as a value judgment.

A picture often looks contrived, artificial, made-up, and fictitious when technique, direction, or manipulation is obvious. It takes a lot of skill and professional know-how to make these determining factors invisible, and make a picture look like a simple snapshot, a registration of reality, which has always been my goal. *Le Naturel*, as a Frenchman would say.

Technique does not equal vision. Work as mentioned above is in fact part of a research into the technical possibilities of the medium, regarding form, instead rather than content. Consequently. it belongs in the classrooms of an art school or academy and not in an exhibition in a museum or gallery.

Another argument to put a photographer in the spotlight, is that *the artist* - it's hard for me to get used to, but that's what a photographer is called nowadays, *artist* – is working in an *innovative* way or that he's *exploring boundaries*. Consider the person who recently won a photography award for his cut and paste works of art, existing of many digital layers of separate pictures, images that immediately reminded me of the collages Hannah Höch made almost a hundred years ago, with the aid of a pair of scissors and some glue.

The difference with Höch, however, is that, considering the recent work, you get the impression that only *form* is important and that *content* does not count, an issue that has also has been the case in other expositions with titles such as *The Renaissance of Photography*.

The main context of the stunts and masterpieces that are shown is usually the digital technique used to achieve the final result, while we are still dealing with very familiar, straightforward approaches.

Putting lots of pictures together into one image with the aid of a computer is a totally different discipline, comparable with traditional collage, how colourful or impressive the final result might be, and has nothing to do with the essence of photography – releasing the shutter at the right moment to capture a subjective image of reality, or, here he comes again, as Edward Steichen once said: "When that shutter clicks, anything else that can be done afterwards is not worth consideration."

To award an artist who's making collages with a prize for photography is like cheering for someone who scores a goal during a football match by throwing a ball, by hand, hard and impossible to stop, into the goal.

Technical experiments and innovating approaches can, when fitting within the content, support that content, but usually they're only about form and we are still dealing with portraits, still lives, landscapes, and naked girls. They just look a little different.

They merely communicate that the images in which they are used are hip and contemporary and, for this very reason, subject to fashion. Before you know they're passé again.

I often get the impression that *innovative photography* is mainly about to what degree the concept appeals to the spectator rather than a believable, significant, moving or striking depiction of the subject. In some cases I ask myself if we're still talking about photography or about conceptual art *using* photography.

I think for instance of the frivolous sculptures of Lorenzo Vitturi or the work of Wassink and Lundgren, particularly when I see a couple of hardly impressive, quite flat looking pictures of some chunks of soil covered with wheat by the latter. One chunk came from a nearby city park, another from a suburb, a third from somewhere else, and so on. In an accompanying leaflet one could read what the different chunks would cost by the square meter. The difference between them was enormous. Something you don't see in the pictures. It's written down in a separate little booklet: registration with an explanation.

Apart from the fact that this is old news that might surprise a single individual, it has absolutely nothing to do with good photography.

Innovating photography, as mentioned above, can render an appealing image or, because of the written context, be considered as a joke, or be appreciated in the art world but this is no proof of quality as long it is not combined with a visible, content-related vision.

The pictures *themselves* have to show the context and should not serve as illustrations. Without visible context images have no meaning, or, to quote Szarkowski again: "Photography is in the first place about how things are photographed, what you feel when you look at a picture, not about what is photographed." Things that are written about a picture, however impressive they maybe, come in second place.

Art is a sales argument and has nothing to do with quality or craftsmanship. Someone who's incapable of achieving much as a craftsman can always try to sell his work as art. If it's still photography we are talking about, is something else. It never appealed to me to belong to a group of people who produce vague images that need lots of explanation.

As far as I'm concerned, a good photographer is someone who masters a profession, a craftsman; someone who is able effectively to transmit an idea or tell a story in images, someone who can make a portrait that tells something about the person depicted, whether it be free work or commissioned. That's hard enough by itself, and doesn't need a pretentious label. Time will tell if it will be considered art.

One thing always comes first: a picture has to touch you. Instinctively. Boom! At the moment you see it. Whether it be an interpretation of reality or a product of someone's imagination, meant to hang on a wall of a museum or be sent around the world by *Instagram*, a simple snapshot made with a Smartphone or a digital *Hasselblad* file consisting of a pile of layers. What's to be seen in it or how it's made doesn't matter.

It's the vision that counts. The vision has to be clear.

It is the vision that evokes your feelings when looking at a picture. And that's what photography is about.

References

Edward Steichen / Carl Sandburg: The Family of Man, MoMA, N.Y.C. 1955

Richard Avedon: Carmen Dell'Orefice wearing Pierre Cardin, Paris 1957

William Klein: Simone and Nina, Piazza di Spagna, Rome 1960

Irving Penn: Lisa Fonssagrives, N.Y.C. 1950

Lewis Hine: A playground in the alley of a tenement, N.Y.C. 1909

Michelangelo Antonioni: Blow Up, MGM 1966

Philip Mechanicus, Photographer, Jewish Historical Museum, Amsterdam 2013

Bernd en Hilla Becher: Typologies of Industrial Buildings, Mit Press Ltd, 2004

André Kertész: The Fork, The Early Years, W. W. Norton & Company, N.Y.C. 2005

László Moholy-Nagy: Vision in Motion, 2014

Alexander Rodchenko: Photography 1924-1954, Konemann Pub., London 1998

Man Ray: Prophet of the Avant-Garde, 2005

Diane Arbus: An Aperture Monograph, Aperture 2012

Robert Frank: The Americans / Robert Delpire, Paris1958

Jacques Henri Lartique: Diary of a Century, Viking Press, N.Y.C. 1970

Gary Winogrand: Leo Rubinfien and Sarah Greenough, SFMoMA, 2013

Ed van der Elsken: Sweet Life, Bezige Bij Amsterdam 1966

Johan van der Keuken: Wij zijn 17, Van Dishoeck Bussum 1955

Martin Parr: Last Resort: Photographs of New Brighton, Dewi Lewis, 1986

Vivian Maier: Street Photographer. John Maloof, Powerhouse Books, US 2011

Tim Walker: Story Teller, Robin Muir, Harry N. Abrams 2012

Inez Van Lamsweerde - Vinoodh Matadin: Pretty Much Everything, Taschen 2011

Abraham Lincoln / John Calhoun. Photo Tampering throughout History, 2011

Terry Richardson, Volumes 1&2: Portraits and Fashion. Tom Ford, 2015

Brassaï: Paris de Nuit / Paris by Night, Paul Morand, 1933/2012

Charles Gatewood: Sidetripping, William S. Burroughs, Strawberry Hill N.Y. 1975

Hans Aarsman: De Fotodetective, Podium B.V., Amsterdam 2012

Richard Avedon: In the American West, Laura Wilson 1985

Kevin Cartner: The Vulture and the little Girl, Pulitzer Prize Photography 1993

Robert Doisneau: The story behind his famous Kiss, by Molly Driscoll, 2012

David Bailey: Bailey's Stardust, National Portrait Gallery, London 2014

Henri Cartier-Bresson: The Man, The Image & The World, Thames Hudson 2006

Alfred Eisenstadt: Witness to Our Time, Penguin Books 1980

Joe Rosenthal: Flags of Our Fathers, James Bradley and Ron Powers, 2000

Arnold Newman: Five Decades, Harcourt US 1987

Jimmy Nelson: Before They Pass Away, Teneues 2013

Edward Steichen: In High Fashion - The Conde Nast Years, 1923-1937, 2008

Cecil Beaton: Beaton Photographs, Mark Holborn, Annie Leibovitz, Abrams 2015

Hoyningen-Huene: The Photographic Art of Hoyningen-Huene, New Edition 1998

Horst P. Horst: Horst Photographer of Style, Philippe Garner, Skira Rizzoli 2014

Peter Lindbergh: Selected Works 1996-1998, Assouline 1998

Arthur Elgort: The Big Picture, Steidl 2015

Richard Avedon: Portraits / Maria Morris Hambourg, Harry N. Abrams 2002

Jane Bown. Faces: The Creative Process Behind Great Portraits, 2002

Rineke Dijkstra: Portraits, Schirmer/Mosel, N.Y.C. 2005

Nick Knight: Nicknight, Schirmer/Mosel Verlag GmbH 2009

Annie Leibovitch: Photographs, 1970-1990, Harper Collins 1991

Stephan Vanfleteren: Portret 1989-2009, Lannoo 2013

Anton Corbijn: Star Trak, Introduction bij Brian Eno, Schirmer/Mosel 2002

Victoria Will: www.victoriawill.com

Nadar: Felix Nadar and Nigel Gosling, Alfred A. Knopf 1976

Paul Huf: Highlights, Kempen Pers 1994

Dennis Manarchy: www.butterfliesandbuffalo.com

Erwin Blumenfeld: My one hundred best photos, Rizzoli New York 1981

Guy Bourdin: Exhibit A, Bulfinch 2001

Steven Meisel: Three Hundred and Seventeen & Counting, Mallard / Janvier 2009

Helmut Newton: White Women / Feitler, Picasso, Schirmer/Mosel 1976

Sacha van Dorssen: Sacha, Chene Paris 2011

Cindy Sherman: Cindy Sherman / Regis Durand, J.P Criqui, Flammarion 2007

Stephan Shore: Uncommon Places, Aperture 2005

Jean Loup Sieff: Jean Loup Sieff, Taschen 2010

Mario Sorrenti: Draw Blood for Proof / Jim Lewis, Steidl 2013

Bert Stern: Marilyn Monroe, Bert Stern / Norman Mailer, Taschen 2012

Jurgen Teller: Jurgen Teller, Taschen 1996

Mario Testino: In Your Face, Taschen 2015

Oliviero Toscani: Magnificent Failures / Tommasco Basilio, Goodman 2015

Vincent Van de Wijngaard: www.artandcommerce.com/artists/photographers

Ellen von Unwerth: Fraulein / Ingrid Sischy, Taschen 2011

 Bruce Weber: Bruce Weber / William S. Burroughs, Harpers's Books 1991

Hannah Höch: Werke und Worte, Frolich & Kaufmann 1982

Lorenzo Vitturi: Dalston Anatomy / Sam Berkson, SPBH Editions London 2013

Wassink & Lundgren / Martin Parr: The Chinese Photobook, Aperture NY 2015

www.ingramcontent.com/pod-product-compliance
Lightning Source LLC
Chambersburg PA
CBHW070328190526
45169CB00005B/1791